Careers for
TECH GIRLS IN
COMPUTER
SCIENCE

HEATHER MOORE NIVER

ROSEN
PUBLISHING®
New York

Published in 2016 by The Rosen Publishing Group, Inc.
29 East 21st Street, New York, NY 10010

First Edition

Library of Congress Cataloging-in-Publication Data

Niver, Heather Moore, author.
Careers for tech girls in computer science/Heather Moore Niver.—First edition.
    pages cm.—(Tech girls)
Audience: Grades 7 to 12.
Includes bibliographical references and index.
ISBN 978-1-4994-6105-3 (library bound)
 1. Computer science—Vocational guidance—Juvenile literature. 2. Women in computer science—Juvenile literature. 3. Computer scientists—Juvenile literature. [1. Vocational guidance.] I. Title.
QA76.25.N58 2016
004.23—dc23

                                                                    2014042504

Manufactured in the United States of America

CONTENTS

Introduction

"Less than 1 percent of high school girls think of computer science as part of their future, even though it's one of the fastest-growing fields in the United States today with a projected 4.2 million jobs by 2020, according to the federal Bureau of Labor Statistics." As claimed by Code.org, a nonprofit group dedicated to computer science education, computer science is the highest-paid college degree.

Lizzie Yoo was one of those girls who hadn't thought much about computer science. The summer before her senior year of high school, she was re-searching ideas for ways to spend her summer. Over-whelmed by all the possibilities, she remembered her friend gushing about an awesome Microsoft intern-ship. Clicking through the options, she didn't feel like she had enough computer experience for any of them. Then she found DigiGirlz.

She applied to and then attended DigiGirlz High Tech Camp for Girls and had a blast meeting female computer science role models. She got to take part in some hands-on computer science projects, too, such as a smartphone-based scavenger hunt and designing an app. Finally, she met some female college students studying similar subjects and listened to them talk about studying and working in a male-dominated field. It was during this encouraging and empowering discussion that she knew she wanted to learn to write code. "DigiGirlz helped me realize the importance of

Anyone can learn computer science—especially girls. Taking a class or attending a summer camp can be a fun and an informative way to get some coding or other computing experience.

keeping an open mind for new opportunities, especially if they challenge me to step beyond my comfort zone," she wrote on the *Corporate Citizenship* blog. "That said, I'll continue to explore possibilities in technology, with taking AP Computer Science as a start."

Many people believe that computer science is a career just for men or math geniuses and geeks. But new programs, such as some that are in place throughout Maryland and Virginia, aim to change that perspective. Computer science can be learned by anyone, just as anyone can learn to read. Some Maryland schools are working with Code.org, which is determined to encourage and teach girls to code and to offer interesting computer science classes. "We really believe the skills they will get from coding will help them in whatever career they choose," explains Kimberly Hill, Charles County superintendent.

According to Code.org, "Computer science is a foundational field for all twenty-first century careers. All students can benefit from studying the basics of computer science, regardless of whether they want to be a doctor, politician, entrepreneur, musician, or astronaut." You're probably reading this resource because you're already fascinated by some aspect of computer science, but should you decide on another career down the line, your computer science skills can still lead to your success in that field.

Computer science includes a lot of different career options. This resource discusses some of the major job options out there, such as computer and information research scientist, computer network architect, information security analyst, software developer, web developer, and even a little about the career of a video game developer and designer. As you will discover, there's plenty to explore in the field of computer science.

Chapter one

COOL GIRLS IN COMPUTER SCIENCE

C omputers, smartphones, and apps are commonplace, and it's computer scientists who bring them to people so that they can be entertained and communicate. Computer science brings individuals the newest, most innovative gadgets and technologies. According to Teach for America, however, of all the career options in STEM, which stands for "science, technology, engineering, and mathematics," one of the most commonly overlooked subjects in grades K–12 is computer science.

According to the Educator's Room, by 2020 there could be more than one hundred thousand jobs available in computing. That's far beyond the number of college graduates who have the abilities to work in the field. Fortunately for budding computer scientists, one of the beauties of a career in computer science is that there is such a variety of options. Computer science careers range from designing websites, preventing hackers from illegally breaking into websites and stealing information, and creating imaginative computer code and software.

WHAT THEY DO

With so much technology in so many parts of people's lives, it's a great time to investigate computer science careers. Whether it's hardware, software, or other applications, businesses, the military, and everyday consumers all take advantage of the work of computer scientists. In general, according to the website ComputerScienceOnline.org, "Computer scientists code software, build components, figure out how to handle massive amounts of data, create websites, and even solve crimes."

MIDDLE SCHOOL AND EVEN EARLIER

It's never too early to start trying out and learning computer science. Just as young kids have a knack for learning a foreign language, they are also likely to grasp ideas and vocabulary without much trouble. Fourth or fifth grade can be a great time for younger students to try out some computer science, but if students show an interest when they're younger, that's great, too. As long as the concepts are clear and easy to understand, they can start putting them to use.

One of the best ways for young people to start learning these skills is just to start doing it. Similar to learning to play a sport, such as basketball, young people will learn best if they start working with an actual ball. Check out programs that teach the basics. For example, Daisy the Dinosaur, an app for iPads, is geared toward teaching programming essentials to the youngest coders.

Summer camps are great ways for students to immerse themselves fully in the world of computer science, whereas online resources are a great way to start learning some skills. For example, CodeEd is a nonprofit organization that starts teaching girls who are in sixth grade the basic principles of computer science and programming. Another program, called Scratch, was developed by the Massachusetts Institute of Technology (MIT). Students learn computer science skills as they create interactive stories, games, and animations. Then they can share these projects online. Scratch is geared toward students who are between the ages of eight and sixteen, but anyone can use it.

The Hour of Code website (http://hourofcode.com/us) offers coding opportunities for anyone, experienced or not. Users follow self-guided tutorials on their own or during organized sessions.

Students in middle school have additional options open to them as more middle schools include computer science in their teaching. Students use games to learn. For example, CodeAvengers. com teaches kids how to use JavaScript to create their very own video games. Young teens can try out introductory tutorials, too, in subjects such as programming and graphics.

One way to jump right into the world of computer science could be to try to design a website. Building a website teaches important skills such as the HTML (hypertext markup language) computer language and JavaScript. Head to the Code Avengers website for some basics that can be learned online. Students can work at their own pace.

HONING SKILLS IN HIGH SCHOOL

High school is an excellent time to get started honing the skills needed to prepare for a career in the computer science field. For starters, many schools offer some standard classes as well as vocational-technical (vo-tech) courses that will come in handy for students who are ready to get started. Certain schools offer advanced placement (AP) computer science classes. Some classes to consider taking include mathematics, laboratory science, calculus, statistics, and physics, just to name a few. Computer science classes might include web design courses, Visual Basic courses, C++, database management, even information assurance and security, and fundamentals of information technology (IT). Unfortunately, not all schools offer classes in computer science, but as this field continues to grow and increase in popularity, more of them will.

Some high schools offer vocational training or vo-tech classes. Some schools offer two-year (nine-hundred-hour) computer science programs for teens through which they can learn different programing languages and apply them. Certain schools work with local colleges to give students college credit for completing the vo-tech program. Some programs provide internships as well. For these programs students should know how to use desktop computers and be familiar with basic programs such as Microsoft Word and Excel.

Check out classes at local community colleges, too. High school students can earn college credit for taking

Today, high schools are adding computer science classes to their curricula. Students can enroll in vocational training programs or work with colleges for college credit.

these classes—and sometimes do so for a lower cost or even for free. For example, the computer science and engineering departments of the University of Michigan offer a nonresidential summer program called MiBytes at which students complete hands-on projects to learn about computer science as well as engineering. They can build their own mobile app. At the end of the program, they can show off their fun projects at a design expo.

ONLINE OPTIONS

Not all high schools offer computer science classes, but don't worry. Just power up a computer, and with a few clicks anyone can check out some projects, tutorials, games, and classes online.

CODECADEMY

Want to learn to code? Try out some free interactive projects at Codecademy.com. Users can make a basic website or even an interactive website. Coding programs include HTML and CSS, JavaScript, jQuery, Python, Ruby, and more.

CODE.ORG

Head to Code.org to start learning the basics of computer science as soon as you log on. One easy project for beginners includes video lectures starring Bill Gates, Mark Zuckerberg, and the characters from Angry Birds and Plants vs. Zombies. The site even offers offline coding practice options. During Computer Science Education Week, Code.org hosts the Hour of

Code, an hour-long introduction to computer science that is "designed to demystify code and show that anybody can learn the basics." The Hour of Code is a worldwide event available in more than thirty languages. It offers projects for beginners and advanced students. New tutorials are being designed all the time.

COURSERA

The Coursera education site (https://www .coursera.org) provides all kinds of ongoing classes in computer science and a vast array of other subjects, including artificial intelligence, software engineering, and systems and security.

GETTING CAMPY WITH CODE

Summer camps are another great way to be immersed in computer science and learn a lot. Camps and clubs such as SummerQAmp can also teach students the skills they'll need to get the tech jobs they want. It was inspired by a conversation between GroupMe cofounder Steve Martocci and musician Jon Bon Jovi as part of a White House Summer Jobs+ initiative in 2012. In addition, don't forget to research other possible options like fairs, contests, and computer science clubs.

JOIN THE JOB MARKET

Interested in trying out a job using computer science? If you're already in college, head to the career center. Counselors or other staff should be able to direct you to possible part-time jobs

DREAM IT, CODE IT

During the summer of 2014, Santa Barbara High School students Maria DeAngelis and Anna Brewer were members of Computer Science Academy, which offers computer science classes, projects, and programs to high school students. But these girls took things a step farther: they organized a coding camp especially for middle school girls. They worked with adviser Zoe Wood, a professor of computer science at California Polytechnic State University in San Luis Obispo, to create a curriculum geared toward girls in sixth to ninth grades.

"I once signed up for a 'coed' Java programming camp, something I was really excited about, only to drop out later when I realized I would be the only girl," Brewer explained to Barbara Keyani of the Santa Barbara Unified School District. "And in addition to making girls feel safe signing up, having a girls-only camp lets us tailor the curriculum to be more interesting to girls."

Campers at Dream It, Code It used fun games and animations to learn coding basics. Not only do they create virtual pets and games, but they are also introduced to the kinds of careers available in computer science and technology.

and internships available to computer science majors. Sometimes students must meet certain requirements, such as having certain grades.

Those who already have some computer science knowledge and experience might have a better chance at getting more advanced positions. Check out Vault.com to read about some of the most competitive, but exciting, technology internships.

Jobs are out there for younger teens, too. Those who already know how to build a website, even a basic one, could put those skills to work for a local business. Teens who have more advanced computer experience could help maintain that website. Data entry jobs are always available, too, and are a great way to get more basic computer experience and make connections. Some businesses will let students start working as trainees, which allows them to get on-the-job training and the benefit of working with an experienced employee.

Computer-savvy students might work as trainees and learn on the job. For those who need experience, data entry is a fine way to learn basic computer skills.

If a job isn't a reasonable possibility, anyone is free to help out with an open-source project. As explained by software engineer Dan Kegel on his website, "Most open-source projects work like this: all the developers have their own (not quite identical) copies of the source code. When one developer has a change he wants to share with the others, he emails them a patch." As you become familiar with open-source software and use it, you'll likely find new ways to smooth it out and work more efficiently or make use of it in unique ways. Post a patch for the new version and you have a bit more experience!

STEM SCHOLARSHIPS

Women have numerous opportunities for grants and work-study programs, among other possibilities, to fund college. There are options for girls whether they earn great grades or have a high school transcript that isn't so stellar. For example, the American Association of University Women (AAUW) offers scholarships to women who are striving for degrees in fields where women are not well represented, such as some areas of computer science.

The prospects are there, so get out and find them. Your career in computer science is waiting!

Chapter two

COMPUTER AND INFORMATION RESEARCH SCIENTISTS

*S*tudents who like to solve problems and be creative will appreciate a job as a computer and information research scientist. All kinds of businesses and even government agencies hire these candidates to problem solve and create new and exciting products. Sometimes academic institutions hire them to do more experimental projects, coming up with ideas and models to solve computer issues. Others are hired in the medical field, while still others develop the programs that are responsible for making robots move!

ON THE JOB

Most computer and information research scientists have some basic duties. They study issues in computing and then develop ideas and models to handle them. They collaborate with scientists and engineers to solve particularly difficult computer problems. To improve the way people work with computers, they make up new computer languages, tools, and approaches. They look at the software systems that are common in most computing and then figure out ways to improve their performance. For example, they may write the software that runs the complicated electronics in modern cars. Computer and information research scientists create experiments to try to test out the software for these systems. Finally, they study the experiments' results and then publish their discoveries in academic journals.

Some topics they often study include artificial intelligence, robotics, and virtual reality. Their studies can create new technology, and thanks to them technology has been improved. For example, computer speeds might be increased or security might be stronger. Entire computer systems can be revolutionized and new hardware can be created. Sometimes they help develop entirely new ways to use computers.

Computer and information research scientists are behind cutting-edge technology that helps today's cars run—or helps them stop—such as the computers that monitor a car's brakes.

Computer and information research scientists work more with ideas and theories than those in other computer careers. They invent new algorithms and work on making existing ones better. Sometimes the work is complicated and requires very involved algorithms, which are groups of instructions that tell the computer what to do. Enter the computer and information research scientists. These scientists try to make the algorithms a bit less complicated so they perform more economically. They help create technological advances such as cloud computing. Some who earn degrees in this field go on to teach at the college level.

There are three main specialties within the field of computer and information research science: data mining, robotics, and programming. Data mining involves writing algorithms to find and figure out patterns in large data sets. Computer and information research scientists figure out better ways to organize, manage, and show the data. Sometimes they incorporate algorithms right into the software to make it easier for the analysts who use it. According to the Bureau of Labor Statistics (BLS), "For example, they may create an algorithm to analyze a very large set of medical data in order to find new ways to treat diseases. They may also look for patterns in traffic data to help clear accidents faster."

Other computer and information research scientists spend their time working with robots. They study them and figure out ways to improve their performance. They explore how these machines relate with the world. Some computer scientists write programs that make these machines. Other scientists may work on the hardware in cooperation with engineers that design the robots, testing to see if the robots do what

Some computer scientists work with robots, such as these Nao robots, which can interact with special needs students and help them learn.

they were created to do, such as put cars together or gather information from other planets.

Finally, some computer and information research scientists have jobs in programming. They create new languages that are used in software. Some languages might make software function faster or better just by making improvements to the language that is already being used. Or maybe they'll determine how to make a certain part of programming a little bit easier.

CREATING ROBOTS WITH HEART: TESCA FITZGERALD

Tesca Fitzgerald is a seventeen-year-old PhD student at the Georgia Institute of Technology, where she is studying human–robot interaction and cognitive science. She's coding robots to learn from people, the way humans learn from one another.

At the age of five, she joined a robotics team. A teacher noticed her interest and offered to teach her how to code a robot. Fitzgerald loved working on the computer, using code to plan out a design for how the robot should operate and then getting to see it all come "alive."

Fitzgerald loves the idea that one day robots could be so smart that they could even help doctors diagnose diseases. She told Madewithcode.org, "In my mind, I see a future where we have robots that are smart enough to be able to communicate with a human nurse." They could help human nurses with general duties as well as reduce their heavy workload.

IN THE OFFICE

Most computer and information research scientists work full-time (about forty hours every week) in an office. Sometimes, if they're doing independent research, their hours may be more flexible. The U.S. government, mostly in the Department of Defense, employs the largest percentage of people in this field. Other industries can include computer systems design; colleges, universities, and professional schools (which can be state, local, or private); research and development in the physical, engineering, and life sciences; and software publishers.

The U.S. Department of Defense employs more computer and information research scientists than any industry in the private and public sectors.

READY, SET, GO: CAREER PREP

For this career, most employers look for candidates who have advanced degrees, such as a doctorate, which can take four or five years of additional study after receiving a bachelor's degree. Most federal jobs require at least a bachelor's degree in computer science or a similar field, such as information systems or software engineering.

In this field, having analytical skills aids in organizing findings and determining conclusions. Because the job can involve communicating with programmers and managers, people in this career area must convey ideas and findings clearly. Having critical-thinking skills can help when solving complicated computer problems or when a program isn't providing the expected results. Attention to detail is essential because overlooking the smallest mistake can cause big problems. It's important to be a creative thinker in this job because it requires you to come up with new ideas all the time. You'll have to rethink a project when your first idea doesn't work out as planned. Having a logical mind is important when trying to work through the algorithms. Finally, possessing advanced math skills helps in a career like this that involves advanced computing.

COMPUTER NETWORK ARCHITECTS

C omputers are at people's fingertips almost all the time, but what moves that information from one computer to another when people send a quick e-mail to a friend? This process is known as data communication. Computer network architects plan, design, and maintain the computer systems and networks that make communication possible. Others design telephone or cable systems for the telecommunications industry.

ON THE JOB

A computer network architect, also known as a network engineer, might be employed by an individual, a small business that needs to arrange communication between only a couple of offices, or a huge company that needs offices in multiple countries to communicate with one another. This job requires that the person in this position know the company's business plan, too.

No matter the size of the company with which a computer network architect works, she must know its business so she can develop the most appropriate network for it.

GRACE HOPPER

Grace Murray Hopper (1906–1992) was not only the first woman to program a computer, but she was also a rear admiral in the U.S. Navy. She was a mathematician and a computer scientist. Hopper is renowned for her development of the computer programming language known as FLOW-MATIC, which later led to COBOL (common-business-oriented language). She also helped to create the original commercial electronic computer, called UNIVAC I.

Hopper was so good with computers that after she retired from service with the navy (with the rank of commander) in 1966, she was called back a year later to help the navy work with its computer language. She finally retired in 1986 at the age of seventy-nine. She was the oldest officer on active naval duty at that time.

In 1969, the Data Processing Management Association honored Grace Hopper with the first computer sciences Man of the Year Award, and in 1991 she was presented with the National Medal of Technology.

Grace Murray Hopper worked on an early computer called the Mark I calculator. After a moth flew into it, she created the term "bug" for a mysterious computer glitch.

The computer network architect designs a basic plan and arrangement for the network, always keeping information security in mind. She presents this plan to the company and explains why she thinks this is the best fit for the company's needs, based on the nature of the work, how many employees use it, and their long-term goals. This plan should include all the hardware, such as routers, and software, such as drivers, it will need as well as where it belongs in the building.

It's always necessary to research the newest technology to plan for the updates and improvements in the future. Computer network architects build models to help them determine what might be needed in the future. These responsibilities can include monitoring data use and company growth and security needs. They regularly make updates, and when problems come up they need to put fixes or patches in place as soon as possible.

IN THE OFFICE

The job of a computer network architect generally takes place in an office. Sometimes it's necessary to go out into the field to meet with the users to discuss what they want their networks to do. Later, they may work on the installation.

Computer network architects may sometimes team up with people in the company such as the chief technology officer (CTO) as they plan out where new networks will be most useful. Sometimes they collaborate with supervising engineers and employees who put their designs into place. This type of work may take place out in the field.

READY, SET, GO: CAREER PREP

Besides computer science classes in school and online, some basic skills will be a huge benefit if you're looking into working as a computer network architect. Analytical skills come in handy when studying data and figuring out how that data is going to best help the business or organization. This job requires studying and creating complex plans with precise information about how everything will come together, so it's good to be a detail-oriented person. Interpersonal skills are

Computer network architects must sometimes work as part of a team, while being detail-oriented. They must be able to multitask, examine and create very complicated plans, and figure out how the network will work with the various communications elements of an organization.

also important because in this position one deals with all kinds of people and employees, everyone striving to create fast, efficient communication networks. Communicating clearly and collaborating with others will make discussions about new software or brainstorming problems go smoothly. Sometimes you might be in charge of a group of people, so having leadership skills is ideal. Those who work with large businesses have many communication networks to juggle, so possessing organizational skills is vital.

Usually, an employer seeks a candidate for a computer network architect job who has earned a bachelor's degree in computer science, engineering, or information systems. Some employers look for someone who has earned a master of business administration (MBA) degree. Most MBA programs involve about two additional years of study after earning an undergraduate degree. The program will probably include a mix of classes focusing on business and computers.

A network architect generally has between five and ten years of experience. The person's previous experience may have been in network administration or information technology, as well as database administration or computer systems analysis.

SAFE AND SECURE: INFORMATION SECURITY ANALYSTS

I t seems that nearly every week the news media are reporting about another huge business or credit card company having been hacked. But some computer scientists are busy keeping websites safe and everyone's information secure from cyber attacks; these experts are called information security analysts.

ON THE JOB

In a job as an information security analyst, one's work involves preparing and executing the security that keeps the computer networks and systems safe and protected from unexpected cyber attacks. With cybercriminals constantly coming up with new ways to break into websites and steal personal and financial information, among other data, this position is becoming more and more important.

The company employing an information security analyst needs someone with the skills to keep its data safe from wily hackers. With this responsibility comes

At the Department of Homeland Security, one of the tasks of the information security analysts is to test for weaknesses and problem spots to prevent possible cyber attacks in civilian cyber networks.

many duties. In this position you'll constantly check networks for weaknesses or breaches. When one is found, you investigate why it occurred. The next step is to prepare a report that outlines what happened and what information might have been compromised. You'll install a lot of software, including firewalls and data encryption programs, which help keep important information secure.

Information security analysts simulate, or test out, what an attack might do and evaluate weaknesses in penetration testing. This step tests what problems might arise before they can happen. During this

After performing tests, the information security analysts can install effective security technology that will better defend a company's networks.

operation is where knowledge of hacking skills can be rewarded because it's important to imagine new ways for cyber attacks to occur. A part of the job is to try to break into the very system you're trying to secure. "Attacking" your own system helps show where there are weaknesses or holes where real criminals could break into the system. With these tests, the information security analyst can plan and later carry out enhanced security. When a cyber attack is successful, it's paramount to have an emergency plan in place for how to recover from the breach. The job also includes planning additional

HIRED TO HACK

The headlines are full of the latest victims of cybercrime. Big, trusted companies find that even their top-notch security has been hacked, which means they have been victims of criminals using computers illegally. These illegal hackers have given a bad name to some important skills and activities.

But hacking also has a much wider meaning. Sometimes hacking refers to altering the features of a computer system to make it do something other than what it was originally created to do. For example, computer codes can be changed to make a program do all kinds of things.

In fact, hacking might even help some students get their college degrees. For example, the Bill & Melinda Gates Foundation works with College Summit and the King Center Charter School in Buffalo, New York, to fund the College Knowledge Challenge, which challenges students to create a hack to help other students through the sometimes confusing college application process. The so-called Facebook Hackathon is sponsored in part by the popular social networking site. According to the College Knowledge Challenge website, the challenge invites "creative apps that utilize the unique capabilities of and student interest in the world's largest social network." The challenge is to create applications that work on and link with Facebook to make the college application process—as well as attending and staying in college—simpler, especially for first-generation college students or low-income students. Winners not only collect between $50,000 and $100,000 (the amount depends on the scope of the project), but can also be satisfied in the knowledge that their hacks are easing the way for many would-be college students.

security steps such as regularly making copies of information and storing it in an off-site location before something can happen.

It's important to keep track of the newest technology in security, research new technology and software innovations, and judge which will be best suited for the needs of the business or organization. The best security comes from anticipating what cyber attackers will do before they even try, so being imaginative is a real plus in this position.

You'll follow up with managers or upper-level security staff and make suggestions for which improvements or upgrades would be in the company's best interest. Sometimes it is necessary to help computer users with their installation or system education needs.

IN THE OFFICE

According to the BLS, most people in this field "work for computer companies, consulting firms, and business and financial companies." Most positions are with companies that handle services such as computer systems designs, but others may be in the financial industry, information systems, or company management.

The information security analyst position is so important that you'll usually keep upper management—a computer and information systems officer or chief technology officer—in the loop with regular updates and disaster recovery plans.

Most people in the field work full-time (about forty hours per week). Because a cyber attack can happen at any time, sometimes it's necessary to be on call during nonbusiness hours, such as nights, weekends, and holidays.

Most information security analysts work about forty hours every week, but sometimes nights or weekend hours are required to deal immediately with cyber attacks.

READ, SET, GO: CAREER PREP

Information security analyst is such a new position that most colleges don't have a specific degree for it yet. Some schools are starting to include an information security analysis degree, though. Otherwise, you should consider getting a bachelor's degree in computer science or another computer-related field. Try to have a broad computer-oriented education.

Because this work is so important, many employers look for someone who has also earned an MBA in information systems. Experience in a related field, such as having worked in a technology department, is beneficial because it's important to have a working knowledge of a variety of computer systems, software, and technologies. To advance in this field look into licenses or certifications. One well-known certification in the field is the certified information systems security professional. More specific certificates might include one for penetration testing.

Analytical skills help when studying the networks and computer systems for flaws or weaknesses. Attention to detail is a must in this field because it is important to be alert to even the slightest change when trying to identify cyber attacks. Having a crafty mind is a bonus in this position because you must anticipate what the clever cybercriminal might try next! In addition, one who has problem-solving skills can help find holes and potential weaknesses in security.

Chapter five

SOFTWARE DEVELOPERS

*P*eople count on computer software to keep programs running smoothly not only on their desktop computers but also on smartphones, tablets, and even the alarm clocks that wake them up every morning. Software developers are the imaginations behind these computer programs and the codes that keep these electronics humming. Without software, computers would just be useless boxes of wires.

Software developers have two basic focuses. Some are responsible for creating applications that help individuals perform certain tasks on a computer, whereas others generate the systems that run the gadgets and networks. Software developers may also create the apps and games that entertain people.

APPLICATIONS SOFTWARE DEVELOPERS

As the name implies, applications software developers' work is the creation of computer applications. These may include word processors as well as games. Sometimes they'll be hired to dream up a certain kind of software that a customer needs or that will be sold to the public. They may also design databases or write the programs that are used through the Internet or through a business's intranet.

SYSTEMS SOFTWARE DEVELOPERS

When a computer is running smoothly and everything is working well, that's thanks to a systems software developer. They design operating systems for the computers people use, or they may create a system just

Computer software developers keep computers operating efficiently. They may create operating systems software or an interface that allows people and their computers to work on tasks smoothly.

for a business. Systems software developers are often asked to build a system interface, which is what lets the computer and its user collaborate. Most common electronics, whether they're in household appliances

PROGRAMMING

Software developers create software programs, but it's the computer programmers who turn their creations into instructions for the computer. They do this by writing computer code, or coding. They also test the programs for problems, or bugs, and make sure their coding results in the computer doing what they want. Their work often overlaps with that of the software developer, and the programmers often work together with developers. Usually, employers look for candidates with a bachelor's degree.

It's not unusual in the field of computer science to have several skills. For example, Eileen Hollinger is a producer at the game studio Funomena. She also programs and designs games. She possesses a diverse range of skills, including video production and software development.

Are you thinking about programming? Joel Spolsky has this advice on the Joel on Software website: "The difference between a tolerable programmer and a great programmer is not how many programming languages they know, and it's not whether they prefer Python or Java. It's whether they can communicate their ideas. By persuading other people, they get leverage. By writing clear comments and technical specs, they let other programmers understand their code, which means other programmers can use and work with their code instead of rewriting it."

like stoves, in our phones, or in our cars, are controlled by operating systems created by systems software developers.

ON THE JOB

Depending on the type of software development you choose, the duties you perform will vary. But in general, software developers are involved in every step of the software creation process. According to Chegg.com, "You often spend your days writing source code, which is text that's written in a special language designed for

Software developers are involved in most parts of the software creation process. If you are interested in this field, consider taking classes that focus on building software. Learning how to code will be helpful, too.

computers, telling them—like a super scientific game of Simon Says—what to do and how to do it."

This job requires studying the needs of the project or user and then creating, testing, and developing software that fits the bill. Programmers may write and test the code for the project, and then the software developer changes and tweaks it based on her tests. Sometimes the computer software developers write their own code.

If software is already in place, you may be asked to make upgrade suggestions for what is already in use. The design phase might require figuring out each part of the application as well as determining how everything will fit and work together. In this job you might design the models and diagrams that programmers will use to write the software's code. You'll conduct regular tests and take care of maintenance of the software. To that end, it's important to document every step in creating the application or system so it can be consulted for further reference when it comes time to do upgrades or perform routine maintenance. Sometimes software developers work in cooperation with other computer specialists to produce prime software.

IN THE OFFICE

Companies that focus on computer systems design and similar services employ the majority of software developers. Software publishers are another employer, as are computer and electronic product manufacturers. Applications developers may work in an office setting, such as in a business's corporate headquarters.

This career requires working with others, sometimes in teams, to create an entire product. Just

VIDEO GAMES WITH HEART: ROBIN HUNICKE

Many popular video games are dramatic, but they feature a lot of violence. Or maybe the thought of a video game brings to mind sports games or sports cars. Robin Hunicke decided to create games that were more meaningful than that. She wrote codes to make video games that inspire empathy (not violence) and help users understand how people think and act.

She loves creating video games because the work includes "just about every creative activity that you can imagine," she told Made with Code. "So it starts with writing and drawing, painting, making sketches, and watching videos…thinking about different problems."

Hunicke is the cofounder and chief executive officer (CEO) of Funomena, an independent game studio in California. Funomena is intent on creating games that have a positive effect. Some of its upcoming projects are in cooperation with the University of California, Davis and the National Science Foundation.

Besides being a CEO, she is, according to the Funomena website, a designer and producer, with a background in fine art, computer science, and applied game studies. She was also honored in 2014 with the Microsoft Women in Gaming Ambassador Award.

creating gaming software involves producers, game designers, programmers, artists and animators, sound designers, and game testers. Sometimes this job can be done away from the office, which is called telecommuting.

READY, SET, GO: CAREER PREP

Most employers look for software developers who have a bachelor's degree in computer science or a related field, such as software engineering. Make sure to take classes that focus on building software. Some employers want their employees to have a master's degree. Knowing how to code is not essential, but computer coding skills can give you a real advantage in this field. During college, an internship can be an excellent learning opportunity and show potential employers you've had some work experience. Once on the job, advancement opportunities are out there. One common promotion from software developer is to IT project manager or computer and information systems manager. In this job, you'll manage software development from start to finish.

Having some basic career skills will be a benefit in this line of work, as in many. An analytical mind can help when figuring out exactly what users need and how to create software to make solutions become reality. Because you're often working with others, good communication skills are very important in this position, too. Of course, computer skills and knowledge are crucial here, but so is creativity when it comes time to dream up new and unique software for clients. Communication and customer-service skills are useful when explaining how everything works and answering questions along the way. Similarly, when multiple people from different departments or the members of a team are working together, having interpersonal skills can aid in communicating smoothly, especially when there is a lot going on and

Many people help create gaming software. Artists and animators (shown here) work on the characters, but the work also includes producers, game designers, programmers, sound designers, and game testers.

important details need to be conveyed. Giving unclear instructions can mean the difference between having a successful software program and a useless batch of code. It's also important to possess solid problem-solving skills for when that software isn't working well or a new challenge arises.

ON SITE: WEB DEVELOPERS

A website has become an important part of many businesses these days. The image, or look, put forth by a website is an advertisement for the company, and how well the site does or does not work speaks for it as well.

ON THE JOB

Behind every good website is an excellent web developer who creates and designs it, while ensuring that it runs smoothly, is easy to navigate, and is an enjoyable experience for users. Sometimes web developers also come up with content for the site.

Web developers work with clients or a company to discuss what they want from their website, including the type of site it should be (such as news or gaming), how it should look, and what kind of traffic and graphics it needs to handle. A gaming site, for example, needs to handle the most advanced graphics. Then it's the web developer's job to make that a reality, determining which applications and designs will make the site match the client's vision. Some web developers work on all aspects of the website, whereas others focus on certain details.

WEB ARCHITECTS OR PROGRAMMERS

Web architects or programmers build the basic frame of a website. They want to be sure it works the way it's supposed to. Web architects also set up basic procedures so that others can add to the site in the future. When it's time to make big changes to the site, discussions with management will be necessary.

A good-looking website is a consequence of having a talented web designer. She is in charge of the site's design, which includes graphics and using computer languages, such as HTML.

WEB DESIGNERS

How the website looks comes across thanks to a good web designer. She designs the site and includes any graphics. For example, a site that is selling goods—an ecommerce site—will need to have a good checkout tool. She'll use a number of computer languages in her programming, such as HTML or JavaScript.

WEBMASTERS

Once a website is up and running, someone needs to keep up with general maintenance and updates. The webmaster makes sure that everything is running smoothly on the websites and tests for problems, such as links that aren't working correctly. Some webmasters are responsible for communicating with users when they have problems or comments.

IN THE OFFICE

Most web developers work for companies involved in computer systems design, but any number of other industries may hire a web developer, including finance and insurance, education, and even religious organizations. Any business that needs a website might consider working with a web developer. Although most web designers work full-time for a company, many are self-employed.

READY, SET, GO: CAREER PREP

Web designers can get a two-year degree, known as an associate's degree, in web design or a similar field.

WOMEN ON THEIR OWN AND ON THE WEB

Not all web developers and designers followed the path from high school through college and on into the workforce. Amber Weinberg, a web developer living in London, England, tells TechandProject.com her story: "I became a self-taught web developer in middle school when I started making websites for some of my hobbies. I did go to design school but after I graduated, I realised that design wasn't for me. I picked up a couple of jobs as a junior developer before I decided to go out and start my own business."

Rachel Andrew didn't start out in computer science at all! She started out as a dancer and commented, in an interview with women in web design for *Smashing Magazine*, "Web development couldn't have been a career choice when I was at school anyway!" With a background in the arts, she started out doing web design but now focuses solely on web development, as she enjoys the more technical aspects.

Lynda Weinman teaches computer design tools even though she has no formal education in the field whatsoever. She's taught herself everything she knows. Weinman, as reported in *Smashing Magazine*, credits lots of hard work as she followed her interests "plus added in a little bit of guts and tenacity."

In any case it's important to have experience in web design and graphic design. Not all web developers go to college, though. For example, Kristi Colvin founded her own web design company, Fresh ID, and she is

After a website is up and running, the webmaster maintains it. She runs tests to check for problems or examines links that don't work. She also might communicate with users.

primarily self-taught. She took a few courses at a local community college, but most of what she learned she did on her own. She even taught herself HTML. She told *Smashing Magazine*, "I taught myself what I was interested in, gained experience and, once I had mastered the skills of my trade, offered my services doing that for others. I've been mostly self-employed since about 1993 for that reason."

Some employers look for a candidate with a bachelor's degree or higher in computer science, programming, or a related field when filling more technical positions, like web architect. Those who

Whether learning independently or through classes, when preparing for a career in web design, learn programming languages such as HTML. Paying attention to detail is crucial when one is writing HTML.

want to advance their careers can go on to be project managers if they already have their bachelor's degree.

Most web developers must know HTML very well, in addition to other programming languages. Familiarity with multimedia publishing, such as

Flash, will be another benefit. Knowing web design is also an added plus because some web developers handle the website's appearance.

Some common skills will come in handy in web design and development. Concentration is essential in a job that requires sitting at a computer and writing code for hours at a time. Attention to detail is an important characteristic for successfully writing HTML. Overlooking the smallest mistake can cause an entire website to crash. When dealing with customer questions, one has to answer them with courtesy and provide clear, accurate answers.

Internships and apprenticeships are great ways to get some experience in the field. Unpaid positions abound, but there are also some paying internships. Search for these opportunities on websites such as LinkedIn, but also scour opportunities on sites such as Fresh Web Jobs and AIGA Design Jobs.

GETTING THE GIG

Whether you feel settled on a specific career in computer science or are still exploring the possibilities, it's not too soon to start looking for work. There are opportunities to get experience through part-time employment and internships. This section is a guide through the trends and challenges of searching for work.

THE JOB SEARCH

Before starting the job search, get a portfolio of your work together. Consider a website like GitHub to collect your best projects and demos and have them ready to showcase to a likely employer (or even to be included with your college applications). These projects should show what you can do.

Think about contacting a company you'd like to work for and asking a few questions, such as what sorts of employees or skills they tend to look for. A polite inquiry is often graciously met with suggestions for areas of study or classes.

Head to the Internet to start searching for jobs. Websites such as LinkedIn, Indeed.com, and Monster.com are solid choices for getting started.

Poring over the local newspaper to search for a job is generally a thing of the past. These days, most job listings are found on the Internet. Websites such as LinkedIn and Monster are general places to start looking. You can focus your search by location and field, for starters. Don't forget to ask the people you know, too. Teachers, mentors, and people you've met through internships might have suggestions for companies that may be hiring. And this kind of networking can often help a job seeker get a foot in the door.

Recruiters are another way to find a job. Recruiters are out there in search of good workers to hire for one or more companies. One example of what a recruiter (and perhaps an employer) looks for in an employee comes from Olivia Marsden, a talent scout for ThoughtWorks. On the TARGETJobs website she explains, "I want graduates who take the initiative to teach themselves new skills. There are lots of free online courses available. It shows an employer that you have the drive and motivation we're looking for. Also, we want you to be part of your local tech community, go to hackathons and contribute to GitHub and Stack Overflow. It shows an employer that you're passionate about the industry." No matter what your focus is in computer science, passion and initiative are going to get you places.

RÉSUMÉ, COVER LETTER, AND CV: OH MY!

Writing a résumé can be a daunting task. Plenty of online sites (such as http://office.microsoft.com /en-us/templates/results.aspx?qu=resumes) will help the flummoxed job seeker format a spiffy résumé and cover letter that will showcase her strengths and experience. A résumé and cover letter should include a well-written description of what you've learned as well as how it will benefit you in this job. It's not a bad idea to highlight a project you're proud of in the cover letter, explaining why it inspired you and what you learned (from mistakes as well as successes) while doing the project.

Some employers ask for a CV (curriculum vitae, which is Latin for "course of life"). According to Jörgen Sundberg, a CV is an "in-depth document that can be laid out over two or more pages and it contains a high level of detail about your achievements, a great deal more than just a career biography. The CV covers your education as well as any other accomplishments like publications, awards, honours etc." It might use more bullet points to highlight all your major strengths and experience.

Be sure to use proper grammar and spelling. Always have someone else review and proofread your writing. Even the best writers and editors sometimes miss typos and punctuation mistakes.

Most important, let your passion shine through. If this is work you love, explain what motivates you to pursue this career and why you think this company is a place where you'll do great things.

HELLO, MY NAME IS…: AT THE INTERVIEW

Once the interview is scheduled, it's time to prepare to meet in person. Make certain that your appearance is neat and clean and that you are dressed in a professional manner. Bring extra copies of your résumé and, if applicable, project samples. Even if you're nervous, try to be clear and articulate.

Brush up on your basic skills ahead of time. If they ask you to perform basic computer programming tasks, you won't be caught off guard. You'll be ready to show them what you can do.

In our current computer-centric age, some interviews might not require you to go into the office. You might be able to talk to a prospective employer right from your laptop or smartphone. It seems a little

If you are faced with a panel-style interview, find out who will be interviewing you and brainstorm questions they might ask. Try to make eye contact with everyone and connect with each person.

less formal, but dress and act as though you were right there in person with them. Make sure you have a good Internet connection if you're using a program like Skype to have a video interview.

Another new type of interview is a group, or panel, interview. These interviews can be with a panel, or a group of two or more people from the company, or a candidate group, in which several job applicants are interviewed at the same time. Candidate group interviews, which are less common, might involve group exercises and answering questions.

FIGHTING INJUSTICES WITH CELL PHONES: ERICA KOCHI

No matter how rich or poor you are, nothing matters more than good health. Erica Kochi leads Innovation at UNICEF, which uses cell phones to fight disease and injustice. She was in a rural area of Senegal where there weren't even any roads, but she noticed people had cell phones. By using coding, together with cell phones and text messaging, Kochi can communicate with thousands around the world. Code allows the Innovation program to create systems that connect with hundreds of thousands of people worldwide, even in the most remote areas. By texting simple questions and receiving answers, it ensures that children receive immunizations and treatment for diseases such as HIV. It even helps register the births of children!

FIRST-JOB TIPS

Once you've got a job, it's really time to get to work. Unfortunately, even though the computer science industry is gradually moving toward a more balanced ratio of men to women, women still face discrimination. Doing a good job is a great start, but it's not always enough. As reported by Jennifer Koebele on Computer Science Online, "According to Stanford University studies, women's quit rate in technology exceeds that of other science and engineering fields. A full 56 percent of women in technology companies leave their organizations at the mid-level point in their careers."

SPEAK IT

On the job, it's important to ask for what you want. Don't sit back and expect others to know what you need. Stand up and be clear about what you want and why. Want a raise? Explain to the boss why you deserve it and have concrete examples of how your work is invaluable to the company. Study up on negotiation and some strategies that can help you move ahead.

Even if you're new to a job, have confidence in your talents and ideas. Be sure to communicate your thoughts clearly.

PLAN IT

Have a plan for your long-term goals. Don't expect to reach these goals right away, but having a plan and breaking it down into manageable steps can help keep you focused on advancing your career.

FLEX IT

Just because you're new to a company or just starting a first job doesn't mean you don't have great ideas. It's easy to feel insecure. On the *Smashing Magazine* website, Grace Smith says, "I think part of the problem lies in the lack of willingness among many female designers to get involved in self-promotion. I believe as a whole that we don't tend to bang the drum about our work as hard or market ourselves as strongly." Studies show that most men think they can do it, whereas women are less confident. Speak out with your thoughts, show what you can do, and take on challenges.

KNOWLEDGE IS POWER

When asked if she thought women had a hard time succeeding in the [web] design world, Amber Weinberg told *Smashing Magazine*, "In design school almost every student was female, so I don't think so. I find that most of my clients (agencies and other freelancers) are male, but it is definitely not rare to see women designers, and I have quite a few as clients. Ninety-nine percent of what I do is actually front-end development (CSS, HTML, WordPress), which I think is even rarer to find a woman in. I get comments (which are annoying, honestly) from men that they've never seen a woman developer before . . . it makes me feel like a nearly extinct bird or something." Whether it's web development or design or even information security analysis, it's important to stay on top of your game, especially once you've been in the position for a while. Advancing your education can only help you explore and succeed in a career you'll love.

STAYING AT THE TOP OF YOUR GAME

OK, so now you've got the job. But continuing your education is always something to look into. Much can be learned on the job—from experience and colleagues alike—but there's no substitute for learning about new innovations, especially in a field where computers are constantly advancing and changing. Universities and community colleges often offer night classes for the working population who want to stay up to date or work on a second or advanced degree. Many classes are offered online, which is much more flexible.

It's imperative to keep up with the latest technology in computer science. Online classes make learning more convenient than ever, even if you have a hectic schedule.

Traditional college courses aren't the only option out there, though. Check out workshops, seminars, and the online version of the seminar known as the webinar. Research computer science associations, especially those that focus on your particular line of work. Associations often advertise related seminars, webinars, and conferences. These will all help keep you up to date on the latest news and people in the

GEEK GIRL: LESLIE FISHLOCK

In 2008, Leslie Fishlock got fed up. She was tired of hearing about smart, educated, talented women who didn't know much about computers and the Internet. So she set up Geek Girl, an organization for women interested in STEM. Fishlock says it best in an interview with Jennifer Newell: "The Geek Girl mission is to educate and empower every girl and woman at every age level, on every skill level, at every income level on computer technology with fun and provide a legacy by giving back and paying it forward." She created Geek Girl to bring women together and educate them. Geek Girl hosts everything from dinners to boot camps, giving women a chance to meet, network, and learn. Questions are encouraged and never mocked. And Geek Girl provides opportunities for women to step up and join in by sharing or teaching what they know. Her advice? "Get involved. Get coding. Don't let anyone tell you that you cannot do something."

field. Don't forget about online tutorials, such as those for learning coding languages.

Keep education on the front burner throughout your career. It's not hard to stay on top of the latest developments in your field by regularly taking courses, reading up on the literature of your field, getting recertified, attending conferences, and joining a professional association. Don't forget to research options like research grants, fellowships, and other awards, too.

NETWORKING KNOW-HOW

Networking is a fantastic tool, whether you're in the workforce already or trying to land a first job. In short, networking is sharing between people. They share information or services. If someone decides to join a gym, she asks the people she knows, especially those who work out, for suggestions. That's part of her network. The same goes for when she's looking for a job.

A network is made of people with a common interest. It is the people you know, who can, according to the Cawley Career Education Center, include anyone in the following categories:

- Friends and family
- Faculty and teachers
- Peers and alumni
- Former coworkers and supervisors
- Foundations, associations, and conferences
- Facebook, LinkedIn, LISTSERVs

When exploring your network, make a list of everyone you know. "It is important to be exhaustive

Computer science expos and conferences are valuable places to meet other people in your field of work and expand your network, but networking can happen just about anywhere.

in your brainstorming; you never know what insights, previous experiences, or connections a cousin or professor may have."

Networking establishes and cultivates professional relationships. These can form at obvious places, such as conferences, as well as less formal and seemingly unlikely places, such as in line at the grocery store. Practicing a little introduction for when you're nervous may help if introducing yourself to new people feels awkward.

How is networking useful? One major benefit to having a good network is that it can help you in a job search. Many jobs are never publicly advertised because employers often like to hire people based on personal references. So you never know when you might be chatting about your latest cool coding project with an aunt only to find out she knows someone who is looking to hire someone with your skills.

Share your goals with friends. Someone might know of a job opening or be able to put you in contact with someone else in a similar field. Never ask for a job outright; however, it's fine to ask for advice and guidance.

A network is an excellent support group, too. When something in life is frustrating, turn to the network to talk it out. For example, if you know other people who code using Ruby, they will understand and help you work things through.

Keep in contact with your network. This is as simple as keeping in touch with old teachers, employers, coworkers, and friends. It's awkward to contact someone when it's been years between communications. But if you've been in touch, it's natural to offer assistance and less uncomfortable when you need help. Online social media makes this easier than ever. Facebook is great for making social and family connections, while LinkedIn fosters professional and business relationships.

FIND A MENTOR

Everybody wants to know that there are people on their side, but a mentor is more than that. In business, a mentor guides a (usually) younger or inexperienced worker through the nitty-gritty of the workplace or school. In a male-dominated field like

A female mentor may be a tremendous help and means of support in the male-dominated field of computer science. You can learn greatly from her experience.

computer science, try to find a female mentor. If the company doesn't yet employ many (or any) women in senior positions, look around for a peer who can be a good adviser, such as someone who has worked there for a long time. Organizations that support women in the workplace, such as LeanIn.org, can offer help, too.

The computer science field is looking to diversify. Now the push is to include more talented women and get them working in the computer science world. Nothing is stopping you! Get out there and look for the career you love.

Glossary

ALGORITHM A set of rules or methods to be followed in calculations, often by a computer.

BREACH Break or violation.

CODE Computer programming instructions.

COGNITIVE SCIENCE The study of learning and thought that involves the fields of psychology, linguistics, philosophy, and computer science.

C++ A popular and fast computer program that is based on the C language.

DATASET A group of similar information sets that is made up of separate pieces but can be handled as a group by a computer.

FELLOWSHIP An award offered by an educational institution or other organization to fund advanced research.

HTML Short for hypertext markup language, HTML is a language for creating visuals and audio on the Internet.

INTERNSHIP Supervised on-the-job experience for a student.

INTRANET A limited-use network, usually for private communications, that runs like the Internet.

JAVASCRIPT A simple coding language created by Netscape that is often used to create interactive effects.

MENTOR A trusted guide, coach, or counselor.

OPEN-SOURCE Term used to describe software for which the original source code is free and open to be modified and redistributed.

OPERATING SYSTEM The software that controls the operation of a computer.

RESEARCH GRANT A sum of money given for a study, such as in science or technology.

RUBY An object-oriented programming language that endeavors to be easy to read and write.

SEMINAR A class or meeting about a particular subject for conversation or training.

SIMULATE To imitate or pretend; also to create a computer model.

TENACITY The characteristic of being very strong-minded or tireless.

VOCATIONAL Having to do with occupations or employment.

WEBINAR An online seminar.

For More Information

Association for Computing Machinery
2 Penn Plaza, Suite 701
New York, NY 10121-0701
(800) 342-6626
Website: http://www.acm.org
The Association for Computing Machinery provides
    resources to help advance professions in the
    field of computer science, such as publications,
    information about conferences, and career
    information.

Association of Information Technology Professionals
330 N. Wabash Avenue, Suite 2000
Chicago, IL 60611
(800) 224-9371 or (312) 245-1070
Website: http://www.aitp.org
The Association of Information Technology Profes-
    sionals, which has gone by other names since its
    start in 1951, strives to advance the information
    technology profession through professional de-
    velopment, education, and more.

Canadian Computer Society
260 Adelaide Street East, No. 210
Toronto, ON M5A 1N1
Canada
(416) 299-5282
Email: membership@cancomputes.com
Website: http://www.cancomputes.com
The Canadian Computer Society offers information,
    conducts research, and promotes study in all
    areas of computer technology.

Computing in the Core
1101 Vermont Avenue NW, Suite 400
Washington, DC 20005
(202) 349-2333
Website: http://www.computinginthecore.org
Computing in the Core is a coalition of associations,
    corporations, scientific societies, and other
    nonprofits working to make computer science
    education part of the K–12 core curriculum in the
    United States.

Computing Research Association
1828 L Street NW, Suite 800
Washington, DC 20036
(202) 234-2111
Website: http://www.cra.org
The Computing Research Association seeks to en-
    courage innovation by reinforcing research and
    encouraging education in computing by devel-
    oping "strong, diverse talent in the field."

Girls Who Code
28 West 23rd Street, 4th Floor
New York, NY 10010
Website: http://www.girlswhocode.com
In 2012, Girls Who Code launched a national
    nonprofit organization to teach, motivate, and
    prepare high school girls interested in computing.

National Association of Programmers
P.O. Box 529
Prairieville, LA 70769

E-mail: info@napusa.org
Website: http://www.napusa.org
Formed in 1995, the National Association of
Programmers provides information and resources
for programmers, developers, consultants, and
other professionals and students in the computer
industry.

National Center for Women & Information
Technology (NCWIT)
University of Colorado
Campus Box 322 UCB
Boulder, CO 80309-0322
(303) 735-6671
Website: http://www.ncwit.org
NCWIT is a nonprofit organization offering "commu-
nity, evidence, and action" for women who want
a place in the world of technology.

WEBSITES

Because of the changing nature of Internet links,
Rosen Publishing has developed an online list of
websites related to the subject of this book. This
site is updated regularly. Please use this link to
access the list:

http://www.rosenlinks.com/TECH/Comp

For Further Reading

Freedman, Jeri. *Careers in Computer Technology* (Careers in Computer Science and Programming). New York, NY: Rosen Publishing, 2011.

Furgang, Kathy. *Money-Making Opportunities for Teens Who Are Computer Savvy* (Make Money Now!). New York, NY: Rosen Classroom, 2011.

Hanson-Harding, Alexandra. *Step-by-Step Guide to Win-Win Negotiating Every Day* (Winning at Work Readiness). New York, NY: Rosen Publishing, 2014.

Hardnett, Charles R. *Programming Like a Pro for Teens*. Boston, MA: Cengage Learning, 2012.

La Bella, Laura. *Building Apps*. New York, NY: Rosen Publishing, 2013.

Martin, Chris. *Build Your Own Web Site* (Quick Expert's Guide). New York, NY: Rosen Publishing, 2014.

Niver, Heather Moore. *Women and Networking: Leveraging the Sisterhood*. New York, NY: Rosen Publishing, 2012.

Porterfield, Jason. *Careers as a Cyberterrorism Expert* (Careers in Computer Technology). New York, NY: Rosen Publishing, 2011.

Sande, Warren. *Hello World! Computer Programming for Kids and Other Beginners*. Shelter Island, NY: Manning Publications, 2013.

Wilcox, Christine. *Careers in Information Technology* (Exploring Careers). San Diego, CA: Referencepoint Press, 2014.

Wilkinson, Colin. *Going Live: Launching Your Digital Business* (Digital Entrepreneurship in the Age of Apps, the Web, and Mobile Devices). New York, NY: Rosen Publishing, 2012.

Bibliography

Cawley Career Education Center. "Networking: What, Who, and Where." Georgetown University. Retrieved October 6, 2014 (http://careercenter .georgetown.edu/career-exploration/networking/ what-who-and-where).

Chegg. "What Does a Software Developer Do?" Retrieved October 15, 2014 (http://www.chegg .com/career-center/explore/software-developer ?trackid=YBSvl8O4&ii=1).

College Knowledge Challenge. "About." 2012. Retrieved September 22, 2014 (http://www .collegeknowledgechallenge.org/about/).

Computer Science Online. 2014. Retrieved September 17, 2014 (http://www.computerscienceonline.org).

ElRayess, Nihal. "How Hacking May Help Kids Obtain a College Degree." Teach for America, October 12, 2012. Retrieved September 22, 2014 (http://www .teachforamerica.org/blog/how-hacking-may-help -kids-obtain-college-degree).

Funomenia. "About." Accessed October 4, 2014 (http://www.funomena.com/about).

Kegel, Dan. "How To Get Hired—What CS Students Need to Know," June 22, 2014. Retrieved October 5, 2014 (http://www.kegel.com/academy/getting -hired.html).

Koebele, Jennifer. "Women Wanted: Scholarships, Colleges and Careers in Computer Science." 2014. Retrieved October 5, 2014 (http://www .computerscienceonline.org/cs-programs-for -women/#Career_Women).

Made with Code. "Designed with Code—Tesca Fitzgerald." Retrieved October 3, 2014

(https://www.madewithcode.com/article#tesca
-fitzgerald)

Made with Code. "Played with Code—Robin
Hunicke." Retrieved October 4, 2014 (https://
www.madewithcode.com/article#robin-hunicke).

Newell, Jennifer. "Interview: Leslie Fishlock."
Start Up California. Retrieved October 7,
2014 (http://startupcalifornia.org/2012/10/
leslie-fishlock).

O'Neill, Maggie. "Computer Science Before College."
2014. Retrieved September 22, 2014 (http://www
.computerscienceonline.org/cs-programs-before
-college).

Smashing Magazine. "Women In Web Design:
Group Interview." May 11, 2010. Retrieved
October 5, 2014 (http://www.smashingmagazine
.com/2010/05/11/women-in-web-design-group
-interview).

St. George, Donna. "High School Students Are All
About Computers but Get Little Instruction in
Computer Science." *Washington Post*, April 23,
2014. Retrieved September 22, 2014
(http://www.washingtonpost.com/local/
education/high-school-students-are-all-about
-computers-but-get-little-instruction-in
-computer-science/2014/04/23/13979eda
-c185-11e3-bcec-b71ee10e9bc3_story.html).

Sundberg, Jörgen. "CV vs. Resume: The Difference
and When to Use Which." The Undercover
Recruiter, 2014. Retrieved October 23, 2014
(http://theundercoverrecruiter.com/cv-vs
-resume-difference-and-when-use-which).

TARGETJobs. "Why Your Computer Science Degree Won't Get You an IT Job." Retrieved October 16, 2014 (http://targetjobs.co.uk/career-sectors/it -and-technology/323039-why-your-computer -science-degree-wont-get-you-an-it-job).

Tech and Project. " 'How I Became a Web Developer' Story of 10 Web Developers/ Designers-Case Study." Tech and Project, July 20, 2012. Retrieved October 5, 2014 (http:// www.techandproject.com/2012/07/how -i-became-web-developer-case-study.html).

Yoo, Lizzie. "Diary of a DigiGirl: Lizzie Yoo." February 15, 2013, TechNet Blogs. Retrieved October 7, 2014 (http://blogs.technet.com/b/ microsoftupblog/archive/2013/02/15/lizzie -yoo.aspx).

Index

ABOUT THE AUTHOR

Heather Moore Niver is a New York State writer and editor. She has written more than twenty nonfiction books for children and young adults, including *Women and Networking: Leveraging the Sisterhood*, *Dream Careers in Sports Marketing*, *Careers in Construction*, and *Cool Careers Without College for People Who Can Build Things*. She's also written books on the electronics platform Arduino and the programming language Ruby.

PHOTO CREDITS